AF270377

# ADIDAS

KENNY ABDO

Fly!

An Imprint of Abdo Zoom
abdobooks.com

**abdobooks.com**

Published by Abdo Zoom, a division of ABDO, P.O. Box 398166, Minneapolis, Minnesota 55439. Copyright © 2025 by Abdo Consulting Group, Inc. International copyrights reserved in all countries. No part of this book may be reproduced in any form without written permission from the publisher. Fly!™ is a trademark and logo of Abdo Zoom.

Printed in the United States of America, North Mankato, Minnesota.
102024
012025

Photo Credits: Alamy, Getty Images, Shutterstock
Production Contributors: Kenny Abdo, Jennie Forsberg, Grace Hansen
Design Contributors: Candice Keimig, Neil Klinepier, Laura Graphenteen

**Library of Congress Control Number: 2024936558**

**Publisher's Cataloging-in-Publication Data**

Names: Abdo, Kenny, author.
Title: Adidas / by Kenny Abdo
Description: Minneapolis, Minnesota : Abdo Zoom, 2025 | Series: Sneakerheads | Includes online resources and index.
Identifiers: ISBN 9781098287436 (lib. bdg.) | ISBN 9781098288136 (ebook) | ISBN 9781098288488 (Read-to-me ebook)
Subjects: LCSH: Sneakers--Juvenile literature. | Shoes--Juvenile literature. | Fashion--Social aspects--Juvenile literature. | Adidas USA (Firm)--Juvenile literature.
Classification: DDC 391.413--dc23

# TABLE OF CONTENTS

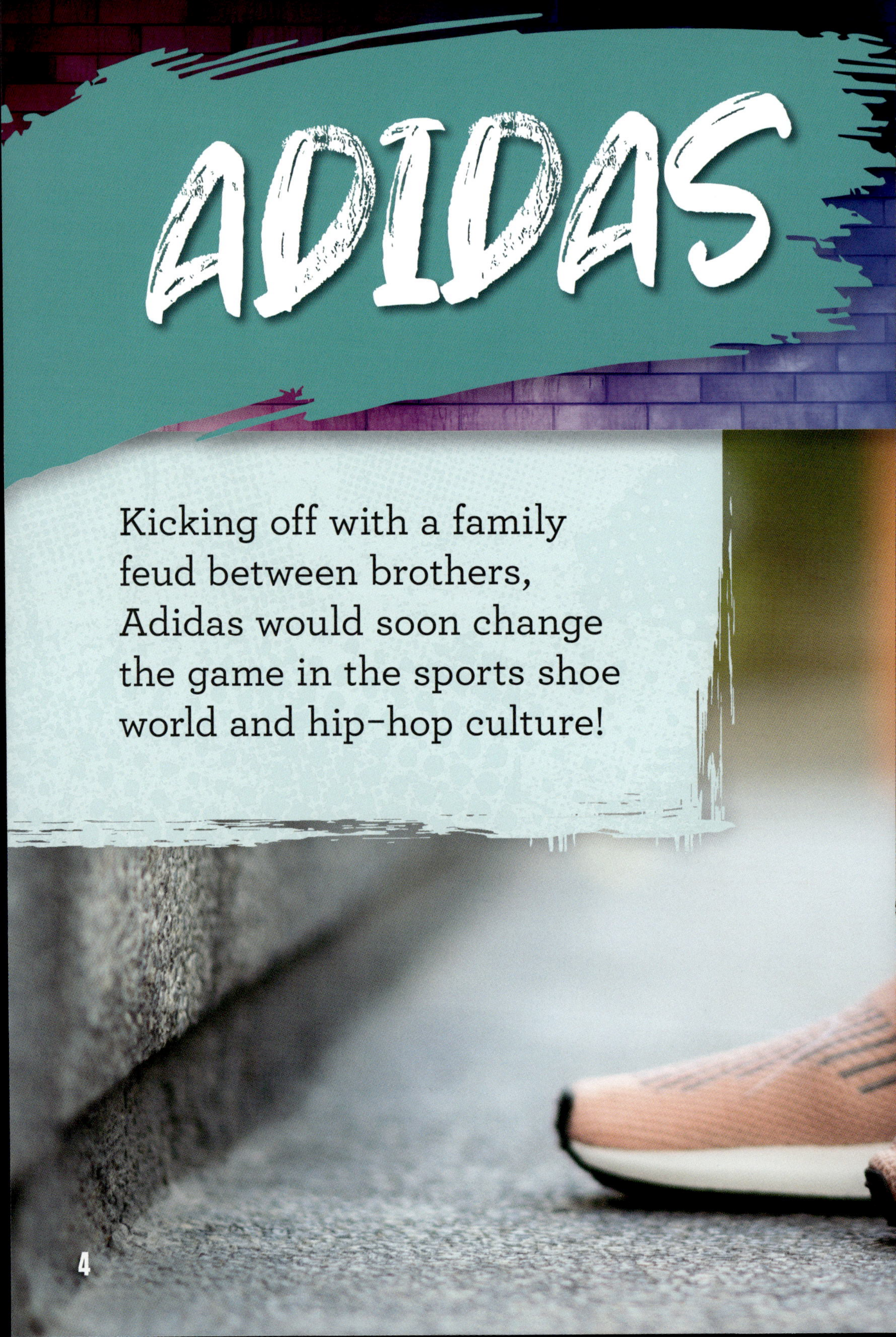

# ADIDAS

Kicking off with a family feud between brothers, Adidas would soon change the game in the sports shoe world and hip-hop culture!

From athletic footwear to ultimate street **cred** status, everyone looks to the three-stripes for style!

# THE OGs

Brothers Adolf and Rudolf Dassler **debuted** their first sneaker in 1920.

Jesse Owens wore a pair at the 1936 **Olympics**. The shoes helped him win four gold medals! They quickly became the must-have athletic sneaker.

After an argument, the brothers parted ways in 1948. Rudolf created PUMA Shoes. Adolph formed his own **brand** called Adidas. The name was a combination of his first and last name.

# THE KICKS

The Samba **debuted** in 1949. The suction **soles** helped soccer players practice on icy ground. The Samba also introduced the **iconic** three stripes.

Adidas went from soccer fields to tennis courts in 1965 with a new shoe named after French tennis star Robert Haillet. It quickly became a staple of the sport! Haillet retired in 1971. Adidas renamed the shoe the Stan Smith after the American tennis great.

The Adidas Superstar took the stage in the '80s. Famous rap group Run DMC **debuted** their song "My Adidas" in 1986.

Sales skyrocketed after the song's release. It also started hip-hop sneaker culture.

The biggest stars in music, skateboarding, and sports laced up with Adidas. Kobe Bryant's KB8 **debuted** in 1997. Bryant made the shoes legendary by winning a slam dunk contest while wearing them!

The 2000s saw the shoe's style grow with the new era. Many **collaborations** with Adidas were also released. The **iconic** Y-3 shoe from Japanese designer Yohji Yamamoto **debuted** in 2003.

During the mid-2010s, the Ultra Boost rose in popularity. The shoes were considered some of the most comfortable in the world. This made them a go-to for runners and sneakerheads alike!

Kanye West shook up the fashion world with the Yeezy 750. It became the trendiest sneaker of 2015 after selling out in just 10 minutes. The Boost 350 **dropped** that same year. The shoes sold out worldwide in one hour!

Though many shoes have been released, the **OGs** remain at the top. The Stan Smith tennis shoes are Adidas' most popular and best-selling shoe. More than 100 million pairs have been sold!

adidas

Today, Adidas is the largest sportswear manufacturer in Europe. They are the second largest in the world after Nike. The company surely gives all other competitors a *run* for their money!

# GLOSSARY

**brand** – a name, design, or symbol that separates one product from another.

**collaboration** – to work with another person or group to do something or reach a goal.

**cred** – short for credibility. In pop culture, it refers to having popularity with the public, especially young people.

**debut** – a first appearance.

**drop** – when something that is highly anticipated is released to the public.

**iconic** – widely known or easily recognized.

**OG** – someone or something that is an original or creator. Usually highly respected.

**Olympic Games** – the biggest sporting event in the world that is divided into summer and winter games.

**sole** – the underside of a shoe.

To learn more about Adidas, please visit **abdobooklinks.com** or scan this QR code. These links are routinely monitored and updated to provide the most current information available.

# INDEX